# Ocean Scientists

By Patrick and Janet Lalley

STECK-VAUGHN
ELEMENTARY • SECONDARY • ADULT • LIBRARY
A Harcourt Company

www.steck-vaughn.com

**ISBN 0-7398-4938-7**



Printed and bound in the United States of America
1 2 3 4 5 6 7 8 9 10 WZ 05 04 03 02 01

**Photo Acknowledgments**
Bruce Carlson, cover, 20, 41 (bottom)
Corbis, 25, 39; Bettmann, 14, 16, 18
Photo Network/Chad Ehlers, title page; Hal Beral, 4, 22, 36, 41 (top); Howard Folsom, 9; Tom Haight, 26
PhotoDisc, 40 (top)
Visuals Unlimited/David B. Fleetham, 10, 40 (bottom); John Lough, 12; David Fleetham, 29, 44; R. DeGoursey; Bill Tice, 34

**Content Consultants**
Maria Kent Rowell
Science Consultant
Sebastopol, California

David Larwa
National Science Education Consultant
Educational Training Services
Brighton, Michigan

**This book supports National Science Standards.**

# Contents

Fish have special body parts called fins to help them move through the water.

# What Is an Ocean Biome?

Many scientists study the ocean **biome**. A biome is a large region, or area, made of communities. A community is a group of certain plants and animals that live in the same place. Communities in the same biome are alike in some ways. In the ocean, for example, plants and animals must be able to live in the water.

There are four oceans on Earth. They are the Pacific, Atlantic, Indian, and Arctic Oceans. These four oceans cover more than 70% of the planet. The ocean biome is the largest biome in the world.

This map shows the location of the major oceans of the world.

## Oceans of the World

The four oceans are sometimes talked about as a single ocean. This is because they are all connected. The waters of the Pacific, Atlantic, and Indian Oceans meet around Antarctica. The waters of the Atlantic and Pacific Oceans meet in the Arctic Ocean.

All of the oceans are different sizes. The largest is the Pacific Ocean. It covers about 70 million square miles (181 million sq. km). The Arctic is the smallest ocean, covering about 5.5 million square miles (14 million sq. km).

**FUN FACT**

Did you know that the levels of the oceans are slowly rising? Over the past 100 years, the ocean has risen about 5 inches (13 cm). The oceans are rising because some of the ice at the North and South Poles has melted. Water takes up more room when it changes from ice to liquid. The reason the ice at the Poles is melting is because over the past 100 years, the average temperature on Earth has risen.

## What Are Oceans?

Oceans are huge bodies of water. The water in oceans is salty, and warm oceans are much saltier than cold ones. This is because the sun **evaporates** more water from the warmer oceans. Evaporate means to turn from a liquid into a gas. When ocean water evaporates, salt is left behind. Since more water evaporates in warm oceans than in cold oceans, the warm oceans are saltier.

The average temperature for the ocean biome is 39° F (3.8° C). The oceans closer to the **equator** are warmer. The equator is an imaginary line that wraps around the middle of Earth. Land and water near the equator are warm all year round.

The oceans near the North and South Poles are so cold that the surface is frozen. The Poles are the farthest points to the north and to the south of Earth. Huge pieces of ice called **icebergs** float in these cold oceans. They slowly melt when they drift into warmer ocean waters.

**These icebergs are floating on the cold water of the Arctic Ocean.**

The bottom of the ocean is called the floor. The shape of the land there is similar to what you can see on dry land. There are mountains, valleys, and plains. There are also **trenches**. Trenches are deep cracks that have opened up along the ocean floor.

Sharks have gills that help them take oxygen from water.

## What Lives in Oceans?

Ocean plants and animals have adapted to live in the water. To be adapted means that something is a good fit for where it lives. Most plants and animals that live in oceans could not live in another biome.

Seaweeds are plants that grow in the ocean. They have no roots, stems, or leaves. Seaweed provides shelter and food for many ocean fish. Seaweed is also used by people to make some glues, soaps, ice cream, and salad dressings.

There are many different kinds of animals in the ocean. Both fish and mammals live there. Fish are cold-blooded animals with fins and scales. The body of a cold-blooded animal warms or cools to about the same temperature as the air or water around it. Fish breathe under water through body parts called gills. Some ocean fish include sharks, tuna, and eels.

Mammals are warm-blooded animals with a backbone. Warm-blooded animals have a body temperature that stays the same when it is hot or cold. Mammals in the ocean must come to the surface to breathe air. Some ocean mammals include whales, dolphins, and manatees.

**Plankton** also live in the ocean. Plankton is a mixture of tiny plants and animals. Plankton live near the surface of the ocean. Plankton is food for many ocean animals, including the blue whale.

This duck is coated in oil from swimming in water polluted with oil.

## Why Are the Oceans in Danger?

People are causing problems for the oceans. People **pollute** when they put harmful materials into air, water, or soil. Many animals have died from eating plastic bags people have dumped into the oceans. Seals and dolphins have died from being caught in plastic straps that hold people's drink containers together.

Chemicals made by people also pour into the oceans from rivers. Some of these chemicals are **pesticides**. Pesticides are used by farmers and other people to kill insects. Other materials, such as toxic waste and garbage, are sometimes dumped directly into the oceans. Toxic waste is poisonous material left over after some kind of product has been made.

The ocean is also being polluted by oil. Some of it spills from the oil platforms where people drill to find oil. When they drill through the ocean floor, oil spills into the ocean. Some of it also spills when tanker ships carrying oil have accidents.

Another way people harm oceans is by overfishing. Overfishing means people are taking too many fish for food. When they do this, some species of fish could become **extinct**.

**Global warming** also affects oceans. Global warming is a slow but measurable rise in temperatures across all of Earth. Even small changes in temperatures can cause changes in weather patterns. These changes mean some parts of the ocean might have higher or lower temperatures. This affects plants and animals.

Jacques Cousteau is a famous scientist who worked to save the oceans.

# A Famous Ocean Scientist

Jacques Cousteau was one of the most famous ocean scientists in the world. He was born in France in 1910 in a town near the ocean. He spent his whole life studying the ocean and the animals that live there.

At first, Cousteau was not a very good student. Since he got into trouble a lot, his family sent him to a strict boarding school. He loved the school and did very well there. After he graduated, Cousteau became a student at France's Naval Academy. In 1933, he joined the French navy and was an officer and a spy.

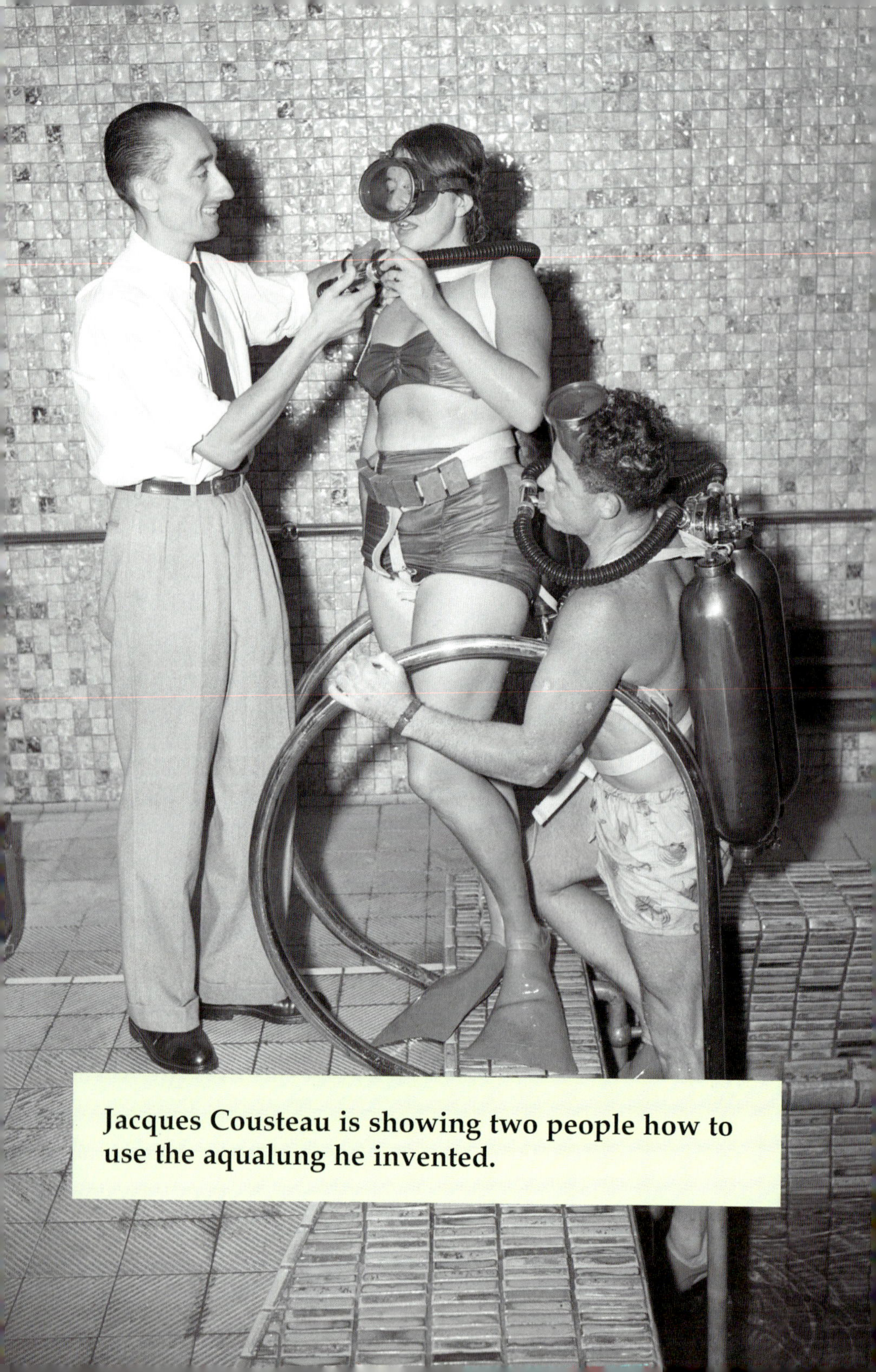

Jacques Cousteau is showing two people how to use the aqualung he invented.

## Serving in the Navy

In the Navy, Cousteau worked on inventing a machine that would let divers breathe under the water. During World War II, he worked with a French engineer named Emile Gagnan. The two men completed their invention in 1943. It was called the **aqualung**. It let divers breathe under water for several hours. Divers used the aqualung to find and remove mines after World War II.

In 1950, Cousteau became president of the French Oceanographic Campaigns and explored the ocean. Cousteau bought a ship so he and the other scientists could do their work well. The ship was called the *Calypso,* and it became as famous as Cousteau.

Cousteau decided to make movies to teach people about the ocean and to help pay for his trips. Two of Cousteau's movies won the Academy Award for best documentary film. The Academy Awards are some of the most famous movie awards in the world. *The Silent World* won an Academy Award in 1956, and *World Without Sun* won in 1966.

This is a picture of the *Calypso* on the Mississippi River.

## After the Navy

Cousteau left the Navy in 1957 and became director of the Oceanographic Museum of Monaco. There, he became head of the Conshelf Saturation Dive Program. The program was an experiment started in 1961. The Conshelf was an underwater house shaped like a big barrel. It was held to the bottom of the ocean with weights. The men on the program lived and worked under water to study the ocean. For the first experiment, two divers stayed in the Conshelf for seven days and nights. The experiment was a big success, so Cousteau did it two more times. The experiments brought people closer to living and working in the sea.

In the late 1960s and early to mid-1970s, Cousteau had a television series called *The Undersea World of Jacques Cousteau*. Cousteau's series introduced people to dolphins, sharks, and **coral reefs**. The television series also helped make the *Calypso* famous. The ship often traveled more than 100,000 miles (160,000 km) in a year. Its crew explored the Arctic Ocean and the Mississippi River. They searched for sunken ships and researched the effects of pollution.

Cousteau did more than anyone ever has to teach people about the ocean. He was awarded the Medal of Freedom by U.S. President Ronald Reagan in 1985. In 1989, his native country of France made him a member of an important organization called the French Academy.

Bruce Carlson is a scientist who studies coral reefs. He is using a camera to film the reefs.

# A Scientist in Fiji

Bruce Carlson is a scientist who has spent most of his life studying coral reefs. He is the director of the Waikiki Aquarium at the University of Hawaii. When he was in high school, Carlson read as many books as he could about oceans. In college, he took all kinds of science classes.

After college, he started studying just coral reefs. Carlson thinks that it is better to learn about a whole subject, such as science, first. Then, you will know enough to choose something you want to learn more about.

This fish is swimming among the coral in a reef.

## Studying Coral Reefs

Coral reefs are some of the most beautiful and fragile things in the oceans. Parts of a coral reef are alive, but most of a reef is dead. Live animals cling to the skeletons left behind by dead coral. Other living things, such as **algae**, are also found on coral reefs. Many kinds of plants and animals live on and around coral reefs. Sponges, snails, worms, and swarms of tiny marine animals can be found there. Marine means having to do with the ocean. Some people say that coral reefs are like the rain forests of the ocean because both places are home to so many living things.

Carlson goes to Fiji to study a coral reef there. The spot he studies is about 10 miles (16 km) from the main island. "The water is very clear, blue, and warm," he says. "Under water, the reefs are filled with colorful fishes, and occasionally we see some sharks, too." Carlson is not afraid of the sharks. He says that the sharks usually stay far away from the scientists.

Carlson rides to the reef in a small boat. The weather often changes daily by the reef. Some days there is no wind and the ocean has few waves. On other days, strong winds whip up large waves up to 10 feet (3 m) high. When the waves are very high, the scientists cannot work. Large waves make diving dangerous.

## Studying Nautilus

One day, Carlson was working near Palau, an island in the western Pacific Ocean. He and other scientists were trapping small ocean animals called nautiluses. These animals live about 1,000 feet (300 m) down in the water.

The scientist trapped them and put radio transmitters on them to see where they traveled. That day, a storm came up and almost sunk the boat. The storm stayed for a week. After the storm, Carlson and the other scientists went out day and night to listen for sounds from the transmitters.

From this experiment, Carlson and the other scientists learned that the nautilus moves from one part of the water to another, depending on the time of day. He learned that the nautilus swims to shallow water during the night. But at dawn it swims back down to depths as great as 1,500 feet (460 m). This was the first time anyone had studied or written about the movements of the chambered nautilus. Carlson says that this information was difficult to gather, but was exciting to learn.

This scientist is watching a nautilus swim through the water.

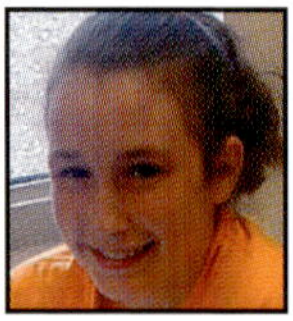

## What Are Other Kids Saying?

Angela Garriott is a 12 year old who feels that we should not pollute because oceans are important to life on our planet. "If we cannot stop, then the oceans will be so bad that we will start to lose our water, and we all will eventually die." She thinks people can help by setting examples all around the world. "When you do visit an ocean, you can always help and pick up someone's trash and your own."

**This is a picture of a healthy reef.**

## Coral Reef Bleaching

In Fiji, Carlson is trying to figure out why a coral reef is "bleaching." Bleaching occurs when the algae that live in a coral leave it. Coral usually looks light brown because of the algae. When the algae leave, the coral looks white. This is what is happening near Fiji.

Coral bleaching happens when the water gets too warm, says Carlson. "The corals are still alive, but unless temperatures return to normal, the corals will die in a week or two without their partner, algae." No one knows what causes the water to get warmer. Carlson uses diving gear to swim under the water and study the coral. He follows the same path, called a line, every year.

"I slowly swim over the line, counting all the corals," Carlson says. He looks to see what things are present and what things are bleached. He writes down what he sees on waterproof paper with a pencil. After counting the corals, he uses an underwater camera to make a video. Carlson says that he returns to the same spot and lines each year to see if the corals are surviving and if new corals are starting to grow.

## Importance of Coral Reefs

Coral reefs are very important to people who live near them. "Reefs protect villages and towns by stopping large waves," says Carlson. The waves hit the reef. This makes the large waves smaller. This way, the big waves do not often reach shore and crash into homes. The coral also brings money to villages from tourists who come to dive.

Coral reefs may also give people medicine. "Scientists are finding that many of the living plants and animals on the reefs produce chemicals that may be important in preventing cancer and other diseases in humans," says Carlson. Produce means to make.

Carlson is afraid that the corals are dying because of the rising water temperatures. He is not sure that the reefs will recover from this damage. Carlson says that he believes very strongly that we need to protect the rest of the reefs throughout the world. He wants to see underwater parks set up to protect about 20% of coral reefs.

This overhead view shows an offshore reef. It protects the island coastline from large waves.

Carlson wants to know how coral live and reproduce. He is trying to grow them in aquariums. People who go to see the aquariums can learn that corals are living animals. Carlson says, "When people know more about them, they will also take more time to protect them."

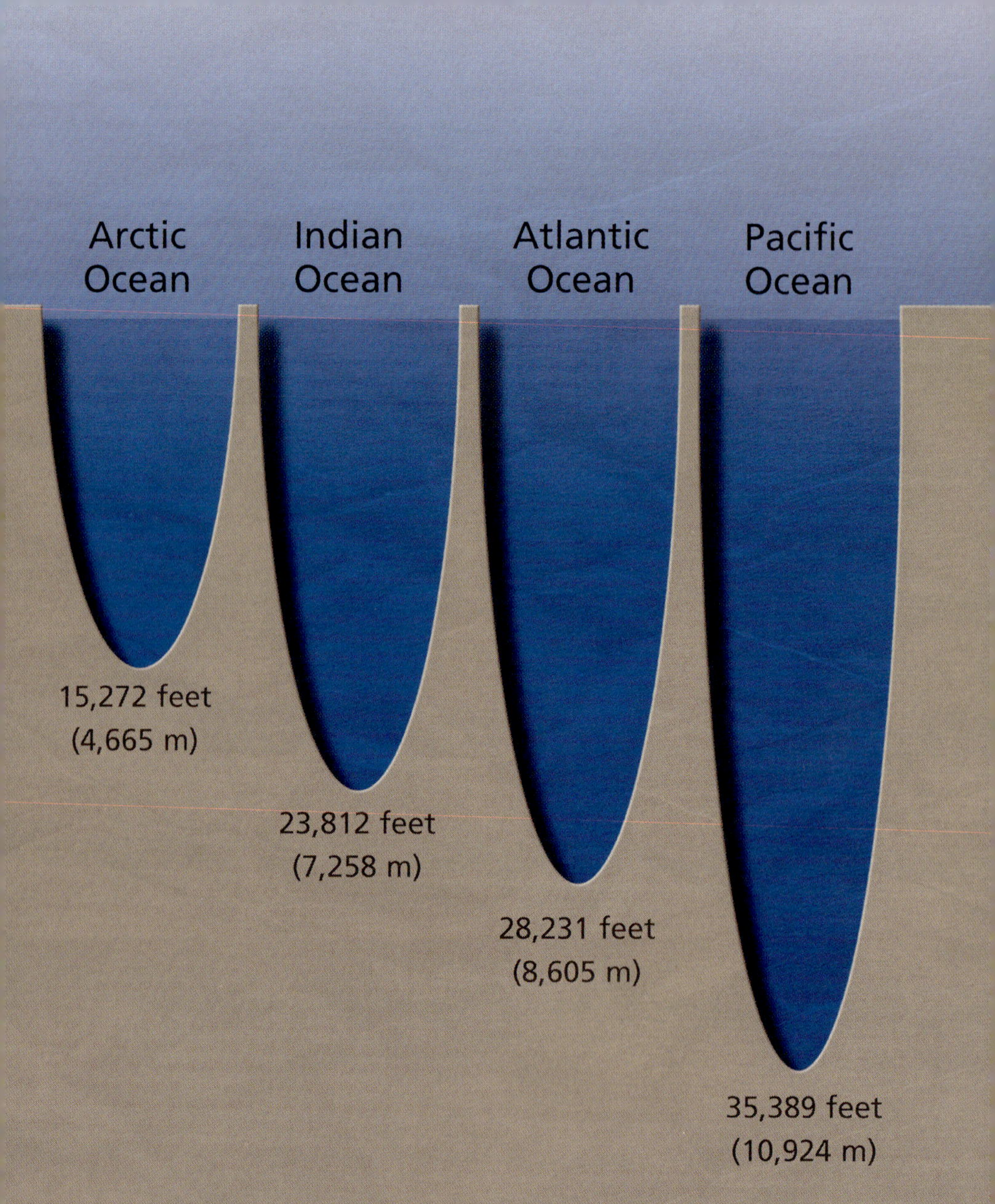


This illustration shows the different maximum depths of the four oceans.

# A Scientist in Monterey Bay

Randy Kochevar is a scientist who works for the Monterey Bay Aquarium in California. Scientists at the aquarium often study deep-sea animals, such as squid. Much of what happens in the deepest, darkest parts of the ocean is unknown to people. Some deep-sea fish are transparent, meaning you can see right through them. Others are odd shapes and sizes.

Kochevar spends time in both the laboratory and the ocean. He uses a computer to study the information he gets from the ocean. "I like the opportunity to learn things that nobody else in the world knows, and I like sharing that information so that we can all learn," Kochevar says.

**Scientists use special submarines like this one to study deep-sea animals and the ocean floor.**

## Tools Used to Study Deep Oceans

Scientists go deep into the ocean in special sphere-shaped **submarines**. Their round shape allows them to go deeper into the ocean than other submarines. The farther down into the ocean they go, the more pressure there is. If they were not sphere-shaped, they would be crushed in very deep water.

Scientists at the aquarium also use deep-sea robots to try to find ocean animals that people have never seen. Robots and computers let scientists study the ocean floor. The scientists cannot go that deep because of the pressure there. They send the robots instead.

One animal that they have not been able to see is the giant squid. Squids have long tentacles that they use to push themselves through the water. Scientists know about giant squids because dead ones have washed up on shore. Still, they have never seen one alive.

Scientists are just starting to learn new things about the deep oceans. Kochevar points out that most of the globe is covered by oceans. "Most of that is deep ocean. If we are to understand anything about life on this planet, we need to understand its largest ecosystem." An ecosystem is a community of animals and plants that lives in a special environment.

The health of oceans depends on people working together to control the number of fish caught.

# What Does the Future Hold for Oceans?

The future of oceans depends on people. Some people are already working to save and study oceans. Other people are trying to make laws to protect oceans. Because the oceans are connected, people around the world need to work together to keep oceans safe for the future.

**FUN FACT**

Did you know that the world's largest chain of coral reefs is in Australia? It is called the Great Barrier Reef. For a long time, only the people near Australia knew about the reef. It kept the water calm for ships in the Coral Sea. In 1768, an European explorer named Captain James Cook traveled there. He brought back news of the reef to Europe in 1771.

This scuba diver is exploring a coral reef that is now a protected marine park.

## Where Are Oceans Protected the Best?

Oceans are best protected in marine parks. These underwater parks are owned and protected by the government. The ocean, the coast, and the animals in them are kept safe from harm.

There are very few marine parks in the world. The largest is found at the Great Barrier Reef in Australia. This park protects the coral reef there. In the United States, an important marine park is the Biscayne National Park in southern Florida. Only 5% of this park is dry land, and the rest is under water. It protects coral reefs and more than 200 kinds of fish.

People visiting the Biscayne National Park can go scuba diving or take a ride in a boat that has a glass bottom. They might see manatees, shrimp, sponges, crabs, or sea turtles. They will also see the coral that makes up the reef.

## The Endangered Manatee

One endangered ocean animal is the manatee. Manatees are commonly called sea cows. Manatees are protected in every country where they live. It is one of the most endangered marine mammals in the United States. Manatees average about 10 feet (3 m) in length. Adult manatees weigh between 800 to 1,200 pounds (363 to 544 kg). The largest manatees can grow to 3,500 pounds (1,588 kg).

Many manatees are killed by people driving boats. Because manatees like to be near the surface of the water, people in boats can hit and kill them without even knowing it. Manatees are also crushed by flood gates that people have built to control the flow of water. Manatees are the victims of poaching and vandalism, too. Poaching means to illegally kill something. People also vandalize manatees by carving things into their thick skin.

People who live in Florida can buy a license plate for their car or truck with a picture of a manatee on it. Some of the money the people spend to buy these license plates is used to help

Manatees are the most endangered sea mammals in the United States.

save the manatee. You can help by contacting one of the groups with an address or website listed in the back of this book. These groups help to teach people about saving the manatee or other species in the oceans. You can also tell other people about the groups listed in the back of this book.

# Quick Facts

Seen from space, Earth looks blue because of the oceans that cover nearly 3/4 of its surface.

The Arctic is the smallest and most shallow ocean.

The Indian Ocean lies between Africa and Australia. It is the second-smallest ocean.

The Pacific is the largest and deepest ocean. It is home to most of the world's ocean life, including sharks.

The Atlantic Ocean lies between North and South America and Europe and Africa.

Many of the fish living in coral reefs have flat bodies that allow them to swim through the reef's cracks and other openings.

A thick layer of soft ooze covers the ocean floor. Ooze is made of mud, sand, and clay dust from volcanoes.

Many of the animals in the ocean look more like plants than they look like animals.

There are more than 50 kinds of seagrass. Seagrass grows near ocean coasts.

On the following pages, you can find sources of information that tell how to help save oceans.

# Glossary

**algae** (AL-jee)—plant-like life without roots, stems, or leaves that lives in or under water

**aqualung** (AK-wuh-lung)—a device that allows divers to breathe under water for several hours

**biome** (BYE-ohm)—large regions, or areas, in the world that have similar climates, soil, plants, and animals

**coral reef** (KOR-uhl REEF)—a raised part of the ocean floor formed by the skeletons of certain ocean animals

**equator** (i-KWAY-tur)—an imaginary line around the middle of Earth, halfway between the North and South Poles

**evaporate** (i-VAP-uh-rate)—to turn from a liquid into a gas

**extinct** (ek-STINGKT)—an animal or plant that has died out

**global warming** (GLOHB-uhl WOR-ming)—a slow but measurable rise in temperatures across all of Earth

**iceberg** (EYESS-berg)—a large piece of ice floating on the ocean

**pesticide** (PESS-tuh-side)—chemicals made by people used to kill pests, such as insects

**plankton** (PLANGK-tuhn)—tiny plants and animals that float or drift in lakes and oceans

**polluted** (puh-LOOT-ed)—when an area has been made dirty, especially with garbage or other things made by people

**submarine** (suhb-muh-REEN)—a craft designed to operate under water

**trench** (TRENCH)—a deep crack in the ocean floor

# Internet Sites

## Biomes/Habitats

http://www.allaboutnature.com/biomes

*Find a description of each biome and information about the exciting animals that live there.*

## Earth Force

http://www.earthforce.org/

*Visit this site to learn about things you can do to help improve the environment.*

## Oceanography for Students

http://www.onr.navy.mil/focus/ocean/

*Learn interesting information about oceans, waves, water, ocean life, and research activities.*

## Oceans Alive

http://www.abc.net.au/oceans/alive.htm

*Explore fast facts about the oceans, information about whale watching, and how seals are trained.*

# Useful Addresses

**Center for Marine Conservation**
1725 DeSales NW, Suite 500
Washington, DC 20036

**Greenpeace International**
Kiezersgracht 176
1016 DW Amsterdam
The Netherlands

**National Coalition for Marine Conservation**
P.O. Box 23298
Savannah, GA 31403

# Books to Read

**Bright, Michael.** *The Dying Sea.* New York: Gloucester, 1988.

*Learn about the animals, climate, and conservation problems of the oceans.*

**Haslam, Andrew.** *Make it Work! Oceans.* Chicago: World Book, 1997.

*Find information about oceans and life in some of the different oceans of the world.*

**Hirschi, Ron.** *Save Our Oceans and Coasts.* New York: Delacorte, 1993.

*Explore problems, such as pollution of oceans and coasts, and learn different ways to solve them.*

**Steele, Christy.** *Oceans.* Austin, TX: Steck-Vaughn, 2000.

*Discover the geography, animals, and plants of oceans as well as people's effect on the biome.*

# Index